NIST Special Publication 800-153

Guidelines for Securing Wireless Local Area Networks (WLANs)

Recommendations of the National Institute of Standards and Technology

Murugiah Souppaya
Karen Scarfone

C O M P U T E R   S E C U R I T Y

Computer Security Division
Information Technology Laboratory
National Institute of Standards and Technology
Gaithersburg, MD 20899-8930

February 2012

U.S. Department of Commerce

John Bryson, Secretary

National Institute of Standards and Technology

Patrick D. Gallagher,
  Under Secretary for Standards and Technology
  and Director

Reports on Computer Systems Technology

The Information Technology Laboratory (ITL) at the National Institute of Standards and Technology (NIST) promotes the U.S. economy and public welfare by providing technical leadership for the nation's measurement and standards infrastructure. ITL develops tests, test methods, reference data, proof of concept implementations, and technical analysis to advance the development and productive use of information technology. ITL's responsibilities include the development of technical, physical, administrative, and management standards and guidelines for the cost-effective security and privacy of sensitive unclassified information in Federal computer systems. This Special Publication 800-series reports on ITL's research, guidance, and outreach efforts in computer security and its collaborative activities with industry, government, and academic organizations.

Acknowledgments

The authors, Murugiah Souppaya of the National Institute of Standards and Technology (NIST) and Karen Scarfone of Scarfone Cybersecurity, wish to thank their colleagues who reviewed drafts of this document and contributed to its technical content, particularly Sheila Frankel, Arnold Johnson, and Terry Hahn of NIST, and representatives from the Department of Justice and the Office of the Director of National Intelligence.

Trademark Information

Table of Contents

List of Appendices

List of Figures

Executive Summary

A *wireless local area network (WLAN)* is a group of wireless networking devices within a limited geographic area, such as an office building, that exchange data through radio communications. WLAN technologies are based on the IEEE 802.11 standard and its amendments.[1] The fundamental components of an IEEE 802.11 WLAN (hereafter referred to as a "WLAN" in this publication) are client devices, such as laptops and smartphones, and access points (APs), which logically connect client devices with a distribution system, typically the organization's wired network infrastructure. Some WLANs also use wireless switches, which act as intermediaries between APs and the distribution system.

The security of each WLAN is heavily dependent on how well each WLAN component—including client devices, APs, and wireless switches—is secured throughout the WLAN lifecycle, from initial WLAN design and deployment through ongoing maintenance and monitoring. Unfortunately, WLANs are typically less secure than their wired counterparts for several reasons, including the ease of access to the WLAN and the weak security configurations often used for WLANs (to favor convenience over security). The purpose of this publication is to help organizations improve their WLAN security by providing recommendations for WLAN security configuration and monitoring. This publication supplements other NIST publications by consolidating and strengthening their key recommendations.

Organizations should implement the following guidelines to improve the security of their WLANs.

Have standardized security configurations for common WLAN components, such as client devices and APs.

A standardized configuration provides a base level of security, reducing vulnerabilities and lessening the impact of successful attacks. Standardized configurations can also significantly reduce the time and effort needed to secure WLAN components and verify their security, particularly if the configuration can be deployed and verified through automated means.

When planning WLAN security, consider the security not only of the WLAN itself, but also how it may affect the security of other networks.

A WLAN is usually connected to an organization's wired networks, and WLANs may also be connected to each other. For WLANs that need wired network access, their client devices should be allowed access only to the necessary hosts on the wired network using only the required protocols. Also, an organization should have separate WLANs if there is more than one security profile for WLAN usage; for example, an organization should have logically separated WLANs for external use (such as guests) and internal use. Devices on one WLAN should not be able to connect to devices on a logically separated WLAN.

Have policies that clearly state which forms of dual connections are permitted or prohibited for WLAN client devices, and enforce these policies through the appropriate security controls.

The term "dual connected" generally refers to a client device that is connected to both a wired network and a WLAN at the same time. If an attacker gains unauthorized wireless access to a dual-connected client device, the attacker could then use it to access or attack resources on the wired network. Organizations should consider the risks posed not only by the traditional form of dual connectness, but also by other forms involving multiple wireless networks. It is common today for client devices to be connected to multiple wireless networks simultaneously, such as cell phone, WiMAX, Bluetooth, and WLAN networks. Organizations should assess the risk of the possible combinations of network

---

[1]   See [GAO-11-43] for additional information on the history of the IEEE 802.11 standard for WLANs.

technologies for their WLAN client devices and determine how those risks should be mitigated. If one or more of the networks cannot have its risk mitigated to an acceptable level, then dual connections involving that network may pose too much risk to the organization and may need to be prohibited.

Ensure that the organization's WLAN client devices and APs have configurations at all times that are compliant with the organization's WLAN policies.

After designing WLAN security configurations for client devices and APs, an organization should determine how the configurations will be implemented, evaluate the effectiveness of the implementations, deploy the implementations to the appropriate devices, and maintain the configurations and their implementations throughout the devices' lifecycles. Organizations should standardize, automate, and centralize as much of their WLAN security configuration implementation and maintenance as practical. This allows organizations to implement consistent WLAN security throughout the enterprise, to detect and correct unauthorized changes to configurations, and to react quickly when newly identified vulnerabilities or recent incidents indicate a need to change the WLAN's security configuration.

Perform both attack monitoring and vulnerability monitoring to support WLAN security.

Security monitoring is important for all systems and networks, but it is generally even more important for WLANs because of the increased risks that they face. Organizations should continuously monitor their WLANs for both WLAN-specific and general (wired network) attacks. Organizations should do largely the same vulnerability monitoring for WLAN components that they do for any other software: identifying patches and applying them, and verifying security configuration settings and adjusting them as needed. These actions should be performed at least as often for WLAN components as they are for the organization's equivalent wired systems.

Conduct regular periodic technical security assessments for the organization's WLANs.

These assessments should be performed at least annually to evaluate the overall security of the WLAN. In addition, organizations should perform periodic assessments at least quarterly unless continuous monitoring of WLAN security is already collecting all of the necessary information about WLAN attacks and vulnerabilities needed for assessment purposes.

1. Introduction

1.1 Authority

The National Institute of Standards and Technology (NIST) developed this document in furtherance of its statutory responsibilities under the Federal Information Security Management Act (FISMA) of 2002, Public Law 107-347.

NIST is responsible for developing standards and guidelines, including minimum requirements, for providing adequate information security for all agency operations and assets; but such standards and guidelines shall not apply to national security systems. This guideline is consistent with the requirements of the Office of Management and Budget (OMB) Circular A-130, Section 8b(3), "Securing Agency Information Systems," as analyzed in A-130, Appendix IV: Analysis of Key Sections. Supplemental information is provided in A-130, Appendix III.

This guideline has been prepared for use by Federal agencies. It may be used by nongovernmental organizations on a voluntary basis and is not subject to copyright, though attribution is desired.

Nothing in this document should be taken to contradict standards and guidelines made mandatory and binding on Federal agencies by the Secretary of Commerce under statutory authority, nor should these guidelines be interpreted as altering or superseding the existing authorities of the Secretary of Commerce, Director of the OMB, or any other Federal official.

1.2 Purpose and Scope

The purpose of this publication is to provide organizations with recommendations for improving the security configuration and monitoring of their IEEE 802.11 wireless local area networks (WLANs) and their devices connecting to those networks. The scope of this publication is limited to unclassified wireless networks and unclassified facilities within range of unclassified wireless networks.

This publication supplements other NIST publications by consolidating and strengthening their key recommendations, and it points readers to the appropriate NIST publications for additional information (see Appendix C for the full list of references and Appendix A for a list of major security controls relevant for WLAN security). This publication does not eliminate the need to follow recommendations in other NIST publications, such as [SP800-48] and [SP800-97]. If there is a conflict between recommendations in this publication and another NIST wireless publication, the recommendation in this publication takes precedence.

1.3 Audience

The primary audience for this publication is security professionals, network professionals, system administrators, and others who are responsible for planning, implementing, maintaining, and monitoring the security of their organization's WLANs and the devices that connect to those WLANs.

1.4 Document Structure

The remainder of this document is composed of the following sections and appendices:

- Section 2 provides recommendations for WLAN security configuration, including configuration design, implementation, evaluation, and maintenance.

- Section 3 presents an overview of WLAN security monitoring and gives related recommendations, including criteria for selecting monitoring tools and guidelines for determining how often to perform monitoring.

- Appendix A lists the major controls from NIST Special Publication 800-53, *Recommended Security Controls for Federal Information Systems and Organizations* that affect WLAN security.

- Appendix B provides a list of acronyms and abbreviations used in this document.

- Appendix C lists references for this document.

2. WLAN Security Configuration

Wireless networking enables computing devices with wireless capabilities to use computing resources without being physically connected to a network. The devices simply need to be within a certain distance (known as the range) of the wireless network infrastructure. Wireless local area networks (WLANs) are groups of wireless networking devices within a limited geographic area, such as an office building, that are capable of exchanging data through radio communications. WLANs are usually implemented as extensions to existing wired local area networks (LANs) to provide enhanced user mobility and network access. WLAN technologies are based on the IEEE 802.11 standard and its amendments. Throughout the rest of this publication, the generic term "WLAN" refers to an IEEE 802.11 WLAN.

The two fundamental types of WLAN components are client devices (such as laptops and smartphones) and access points (APs), which logically connect client devices with a distribution system (DS), typically the organization's wired network infrastructure. The DS is the means by which client devices can communicate with the organization's wired LANs and external networks such as the Internet. Some WLANs also use wireless switches, which act as intermediaries between APs and the DS. The purpose of the switch is to assist administrators in managing the WLAN infrastructure. Figure 1 shows a simplified view of WLAN components that includes a wireless switch. WLANs without wireless switches have a similar architecture, except that the APs connect directly to the DS.

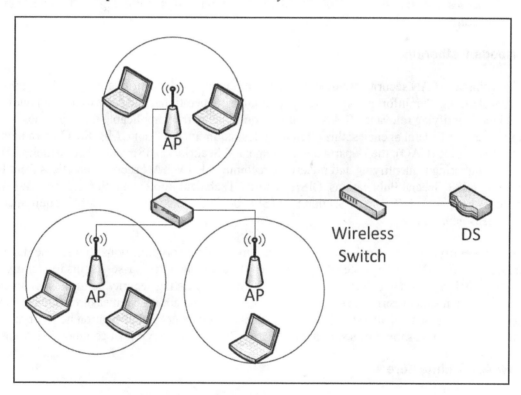

Figure 1: Simplified View of WLAN Architecture

The security of each of the WLAN components—including client devices, APs, and wireless switches—is heavily dependent on their WLAN security configuration. This section explains why having standardized security configurations is important for WLAN components and provides recommendations for designing, implementing, evaluating, and maintaining those configurations, particularly for client devices.

As explained in Section 1.2, the recommendations presented in this section supplement those provided for specific WLAN technologies by other NIST publications [SP800-48, SP800-97].

This section does not provide an exhaustive explanation of the entire security configuration lifecycle; rather, it highlights a few topics of particular relevance to WLAN security. Section 2.1 discusses security configuration design, while Section 2.2 focuses on security configuration implementation, evaluation, and maintenance.

2.1 Configuration Design

Organizations should have standardized security configurations for their common WLAN components, such as client devices and APs. A standardized configuration provides a base level of security, reducing vulnerabilities and lessening the impact of successful attacks. Standardized configuration use improves the consistency and predictability of security, in conjunction with user training and awareness activities and other supporting security controls. Standardized configurations can also provide a large resource savings by reducing the time needed to secure each WLAN device and to verify its configuration for security assessments, audits, etc., particularly if the configuration can be deployed and verified through automated means.

This section focuses on two noteworthy aspects of configuration design: gathering needs and designing WLAN architectures.

2.1.1 Needs Gathering

Before designing a WLAN security architecture or WLAN component security configurations, an organization should gather information on needs, particularly operational and security related ones. This should include identifying relevant WLAN security requirements from applicable laws, policies, regulations, etc. For Federal agencies, this often includes requirements from OMB, the Government Accountability Office (GAO), the Department of Homeland Security (DHS), and other agencies. Another part of needs gathering is identifying and reviewing recommended WLAN security practices from Federal agencies (e.g., NIST Special Publications, DISA Security Technical Implementation Guides), WLAN vendors, and other parties [NCP]. See Section 9 of [SP800-94] for examples of possible requirements to include in needs gathering.

In addition to identifying these requirements and recommendations, organizations should also determine what threats their WLAN security faces. Organizations should conduct risk assessments to identify the threats against their WLANs and determine the effectiveness of existing security controls in counteracting the threats; they then should perform risk mitigation to decide what additional measures (if any) should be implemented, as discussed in [SP800-37]. Performing risk assessments and mitigation helps organizations decide how their WLANs should be secured. See Section 3.1 for an overview of common WLAN threats.

2.1.2 WLAN Architecture

When planning WLAN security, configuration designers should consider the security not only of the WLAN itself, but also how it may affect other networks that are accessible through it, such as internal wired networks reachable from the WLAN. An important principle of WLAN security is to separate WLANs with different security profiles. For example, there should be separate WLANs for external (guest, etc.) and internal use. Devices on an organization's external WLAN should not be able to connect through that WLAN to devices on another of the organization's WLANs. This helps to protect the organization's other networks and devices from external devices and users. Organizations often set up external WLANs primarily to provide Internet access to visitors; such WLANs should be architected so that their traffic does not traverse the organization's internal networks. For external WLANs that do need internal network access, WLAN client devices should be allowed access only to the necessary hosts or subnets using only the required protocols.

Another architectural issue mentioned in the WLAN reference architecture document and discussed in more detail in [GAO-11-43] is dual connected client devices. The term "dual connected" generally refers to a device that is connected to both a wired network and a WLAN at the same time. The primary concern with dual connected configurations is that an attacker may be able to gain unauthorized wireless access to the client device and then use it to attack resources on the wired network. Essentially this is allowing an attacker to exploit a lower-security network in order to gain access to a higher-security network. One possible scenario is an attacker tunneling traffic from the higher-security network to the lower-security network through the client device instead of following the intended network architecture, and thus avoiding network-based security controls intended for the higher-security network. Dual connected configurations also generally violate the principle of disabling unneeded network services to reduce attack surface; if the device is already connected to a wired network access, WLAN access is usually redundant.

Organizations should not only consider simultaneous wired network and WLAN use, but other forms of dual connectedness involving their WLAN client devices. With the increasing variety and popularity of wireless networking technologies, it is common today for devices to be connected to multiple wireless networks simultaneously. For example, most smartphones can use cell phone networks, WLANs, and Bluetooth networks simultaneously, while they are also connected to wired laptops/desktops (and possibly their wired networks) through a cabled connection (e.g., USB). It is also increasingly common for laptops to have multiple wireless interfaces, such as both WLAN and WiMAX interfaces, or to be configured to accept removable media-based WLAN interfaces. A single laptop with multiple WLAN interfaces could have simultaneous connections to multiple WLANs, such as an organization WLAN and an external WLAN.

Organizations should assess the risk of the possible combinations of network technologies for their WLAN client devices and determine how those risks should be mitigated. This does not mean that all forms of dual connectedness should automatically be prohibited; examples of use cases that are often permitted include a smartphone attaching to both a WLAN and a Bluetooth-networked earbud simultaneously, and a laptop attaching to both a WLAN and a Bluetooth-networked keyboard and mouse simultaneously. However, the security of such use cases is largely dependent on the security of all of the networks. If one or more of the networks cannot have its risk mitigated to an acceptable level, then dual connections involving that network may pose too much risk to the organization and may need to be prohibited. The primary risk-related issue to be considered is the likelihood of an attacker accessing and manipulating legitimate communications and the possible and typical impact of such an attack.

Organizations should have policies that clearly state which forms of dual connections are permitted or prohibited for their WLAN client devices under various circumstances. Organizations should enforce these policies through the appropriate security controls, including the actions listed below:

- For all their WLAN client devices: disable all network interfaces that are not authorized for any use (including during contingency plans for business continuity, disaster recovery, etc.), and configure the device so that the user cannot enable them or otherwise circumvent the restrictions.

- For all their WLAN client devices not authorized for dual connections:

  o Implement the appropriate technical security controls (discussed below the bullets) so that all dual connected configurations are prohibited.

- o If feasible, configure the devices to disable bridging (passing traffic between the networks). This is precautionary in case an unauthorized dual connection occurs.

- For all their WLAN client devices authorized for dual connections:

  - o Implement the appropriate technical security controls (discussed below the bullets) so that the authorized dual connected configurations are only active when necessary and that all other dual connected configurations are prohibited.

  - o Configure the devices to disable bridging (passing traffic between the networks) unless absolutely necessary.

There are several options for implementing WLAN client device dual connection policies, such as prohibiting unauthorized configurations from being used and disabling authorized dual connections when not needed. To enforce such restrictions, organizations should rely on automated technical controls whenever feasible. Non-technical controls are usually not effective enough; for example, it is generally not feasible to rely on users to remember to always promptly disable WLAN interfaces every time they are no longer needed. Each organization should evaluate the possible controls for implementing dual connection policies on their WLAN client devices and then choose the combinations of controls that are most appropriate, providing sufficient security while also permitting necessary functionality.

Some of the possible controls are preventative (implementing and enforcing a configuration), while others are detective (monitoring a configuration, monitoring network activity, alerting when a problem is detected, etc.) Preventative controls are generally preferable to detective controls, but it is even stronger to use both preventative and detective controls together. See Section 3 for more information on monitoring (detective) controls.

Preventative controls may need to enforce granular policies. For example, an organization might permit only wired network usage while at their headquarters, but might permit wired or wireless access to external networks. Preventative controls may also need to provide flexibility; organizations often need to allow users to attach the organization's mobile client devices to new external WLANs, and thus the users need some ability to manage their devices' WLAN configuration.

Examples of preventative controls include the following:

- Configure the device's BIOS so that WLAN connections are automatically terminated when a wired connection is detected. The BIOS setting for this is often called LAN/WLAN switching.

- Enable specialized software-based controls that permit either WLAN or wired network access, but not both simultaneously. These controls could be built into the operating system (OS), provided as part of the WLAN driver or management software, provided by the device manufacturer (e.g., laptop vendor), or acquired from third parties. These controls typically favor wired connections over WLAN because of their relative reliability, performance, and security.

- Configure host-based network security tools (e.g., host-based firewalls, host-based intrusion detection and prevention systems) to prevent multiple network interfaces from being used at one time.

- Specify and enforce authorized network profiles and/or unauthorized profiles through OS/domain controls, third party policy-based software, etc.

6

There are other technical WLAN security controls, such as configuring clients so that they will not automatically connect to any WLANs they detect, that are beneficial for WLAN security but not robust enough to prevent dual connections.

2.2   Configuration Implementation, Evaluation, and Maintenance

After designing a WLAN security configuration, an organization should determine how the configuration will be implemented, evaluate the effectiveness of the implementation, deploy the implementation to the appropriate devices, and maintain the configuration and its implementation throughout the devices' lifecycles. Organizations should ensure that their WLAN client devices and APs have configurations at all times that are compliant with the organization's WLAN policies.

Organizations should standardize, automate, and centralize as much of their WLAN security configuration implementation and maintenance as practical, particularly for their WLAN client devices and access points. This allows organizations to implement consistent WLAN security throughout the enterprise, to detect and correct unauthorized changes to configurations, and to react quickly when newly identified vulnerabilities or recent incidents indicate a need to change the WLAN's security configuration.

Organizations can often leverage existing configuration management solutions for their WLAN security configuration management. Many organizations already have general configuration management solutions in place that can handle a wide variety of software; such solutions may be built into operating systems or provided through third-party software installed on their client devices and other WLAN components. Also, WLAN client management software often has configuration management capabilities; this software may already be installed on the WLAN devices. If the existing configuration management solutions cannot collectively provide the necessary WLAN configuration implementation and maintenance capabilities, then the organization should evaluate alternatives and implement a suitable configuration management solution that provides the missing capabilities.

Organizations should evaluate all standardized WLAN security configuration implementations carefully before deploying them throughout production environments. Even if the organization is confident that the configuration is sound, it should still be evaluated carefully to ensure that its implementation meets the organization's particular security and operational requirements. Every operating environment has unique characteristics that should be taken into account. It is particularly important to evaluate the strength of the configuration and its potential impacts on performance and functionality (for example, a security setting that is incompatible with use of a particular application).

3. WLAN Security Monitoring

This section discusses two types of security monitoring: assessments [SP800-115, SP800-53A] and continuous monitoring. Security assessment is "the process of determining how effectively an entity being assessed meets specific security objectives." Security assessments are typically performed periodically, such as annually or quarterly, and are often called periodic assessments. Continuous monitoring is defined in [SP800-137] as "maintaining ongoing awareness of information security, vulnerabilities, and threats to support organizational risk management decisions. The objective is to conduct ongoing monitoring of the security of an organization's networks, information, and systems, and respond by accepting, avoiding/rejecting, transferring/sharing, or mitigating risk as situations change." Think of continuous monitoring as doing assessments in near real-time, so that the organization can react to problems in minutes instead of months or years.

For WLAN security, the same tools are often useful for both periodic assessments and continuous monitoring. These forms of monitoring are used to ensure that each WLAN component's security configuration meets the organization's requirements (and to report all deviations from these requirements), as well as to monitor WLAN activity to identify attacks, improperly secured communications, and other WLAN security issues. This section provides recommendations for WLAN security monitoring (both periodic assessments and continuous monitoring).

As explained in Section 1.2, the recommendations presented in this section supplement those provided for specific WLAN technologies by other NIST publications [SP800-48, SP800-97], as well as NIST publications on general security assessment [SP800-115, SP800-53A] and continuous monitoring [SP800-137].

3.1 WLAN Security Monitoring Basics

Security monitoring is important for all systems and networks, but it is generally even more important for WLANs. WLANs and wired networks have the same security objectives and face the same general types of threats, but WLAN security is typically harder to achieve for several reasons.

First, WLANs tend to be easier for attackers to access than wired networks. The most significant difference between protecting WLANs and wired networks is the relative ease of intercepting wireless network transmissions and inserting new or altered transmissions from what is presumed to be the authentic source. To monitor traffic on a wired network, an attacker would have to gain physical access to the network or remotely compromise systems on the network; for a WLAN, an attacker simply needs to be within range of the wireless transmissions. (Some attackers use highly sensitive directional antennas, which can greatly extend the effective range of attack beyond the standard WLAN range.)

Second, WLANs are often poorly secured. For example, many WLANs are configured so that they do not require strong authentication; this makes it much easier, sometimes trivial, for attackers within range of the WLAN to successfully gain access to it. These configurations are often used because they are more convenient for users and administrators, but they often put the transmitted information and WLAN devices at serious risk of compromise.

Third, WLANs are usually connected to an organization's wired networks. This means that the WLANs and WLAN devices are not only subject to WLAN-specific attacks, but also nearly all the attacks that wired networks and devices on those networks face.

To support WLAN security, organizations should perform both attack monitoring and vulnerability monitoring. Sections 3.1.1 and 3.1.2 provide more information on these, respectively.

3.1.1 Attack Monitoring

Organizations should continuously monitor their WLANs for both WLAN-specific and general (wired network) attacks. The latter involves the same security controls as would be used for any network-connected system in an organization; see [SP800-53] for additional information on general system security and [SP800-94] for general information on attack detection technologies. Further discussion of general (non-wireless) attack monitoring is out of the scope of this publication.

WLAN-specific attacks can typically be divided into two types: passive and active. These attack classes, which are significant for monitoring purposes, are described below.

- **Passive attack:** an attack in which an unauthorized party only monitors WLAN communications; the attacker does not generate, alter, or disrupt WLAN communications. There are two types of passive attacks:

  o **Eavesdropping.** The attacker monitors WLAN data transmissions for message content.

  o **Traffic analysis** (also known as traffic flow analysis). The attacker gains intelligence by monitoring the transmissions for patterns of communication. A considerable amount of information is contained in the flow of messages between communicating parties.

- **Active attack:** an attack in which an unauthorized party generates, alters, or disrupts WLAN communications. Active attacks may take the form of one of the following types:

  o **Masquerading.** The attacker impersonates an authorized user to gain access to certain unauthorized privileges.

  o **Replay.** The attacker monitors transmissions (passive attack) and retransmits messages posing as the legitimate user.

  o **Message modification.** The attacker alters a legitimate message by deleting, adding to, changing, or reordering the message.

  o **Denial of service (DoS).** A DoS can occur inadvertently, such as other electronic devices causing interference, or it can occur intentionally, such as an attacker sending large numbers of messages at a high rate to flood the WLAN.

  o **Misappropriation.** The attacker steals or makes other unauthorized use of WLAN services.

A form of active attack that is particularly noteworthy is the deployment of rogue WLAN devices. For example, an attacker deploys an AP that has been configured to appear as part of an organization's WLAN infrastructure. This can provide a backdoor into the wired network, bypassing perimeter security mechanisms, such as firewalls. In addition, if client devices inadvertently connect to the rogue AP, the attacker can view and manipulate the client devices' communications (e.g., man-in-the-middle attacks), as well as potentially gaining access to the client devices themselves.

Monitoring WLAN-specific attacks is focused on active attacks. Because passive attacks strictly involve intercepting radio transmissions and do not generate their own transmissions, there is nothing for an organization to monitor electronically. However, all forms of active attack mentioned above can be detected through monitoring. Section 3.2 discusses tools that can monitor for active attacks.

3.1.2 Vulnerability Monitoring

Organizations should do largely the same vulnerability monitoring for WLAN components that they do for any other software: identifying patches and applying them, and verifying security configuration settings and adjusting them as needed (see Section 2). These actions should be performed at least as often for WLAN components as they are for the organization's equivalent wired systems. Further discussion of these general vulnerability monitoring techniques is outside the scope of this publication.

In addition to the general vulnerability monitoring, WLAN-specific vulnerability monitoring involves analyzing WLAN communications and identifying policy violations, such as communications using the wrong protocols, encryption key lengths, etc. This is effective at identifying misconfigured WLAN devices as well as devices that are acting differently than their configuration indicates. It is especially helpful when not all of the WLAN devices are under the organization's control, such as visitor laptops, and when unauthorized WLAN devices are a concern (e.g., an employee attaching a personal mobile device to an organization WLAN without authorization). This form of vulnerability monitoring is often provided by the same tools that are effective at attack monitoring, as explained in Section 3.2.

3.2 Monitoring Tools

One of the primary tools for WLAN security monitoring is a wireless intrusion detection and prevention system (WIDPS). A WIDPS has sensors placed at designated locations within an organization's facilities; these sensors monitor WLAN bands and channels to sample traffic, allowing them to identify WLAN attacks and some WLAN vulnerabilities. WIDPS sensors are available in several forms:

- **Dedicated.** A dedicated sensor performs WIDPS functions but does not pass network traffic from source to destination. Dedicated sensors are often completely passive, simply sniffing WLAN traffic. Some dedicated sensors analyze the traffic they monitor, while other sensors forward the traffic to a management server for analysis. The sensor is typically connected to a wired network. Dedicated sensors are usually designed for one of two deployment types:

  - **Fixed**—the sensor is deployed to a particular location. Fixed sensors usually depend on the organization's infrastructure for power, wired network access, and other resources.

  - **Mobile**—the sensor is designed to be portable so it can be used from multiple locations or while in motion. For example, a security administrator could use a mobile sensor while walking through an organization's buildings to find rogue APs.

- **Bundled.** Many APs and wireless switches offer some WIDPS capabilities as a secondary function.

In addition to these hardware-based forms, there are also host-based WIDPS sensor software products that can be installed on WLAN client devices. The sensor software detects WLAN attacks within range of the client device, as well as WLAN vulnerabilities of the client device, and reports this information to WIDPS management servers. The sensor software may also be able to enforce WLAN security policies. See [SP800-94] for more information on all forms of WIDPS.

Another primary tool for WLAN security monitoring is a WLAN scanner. A passive WLAN scanning tool captures WLAN traffic being transmitted within the range of the tool's antenna. Most passive tools record the key attributes of discovered WLAN devices. This information can be used to identify WLAN vulnerabilities and to detect potential rogue devices. WLAN scanning tools used to conduct completely passive scans transmit no data, nor do the tools in any way affect the operation of deployed WLAN devices. By not transmitting data, a passive scanning tool remains undetected by malicious users and other devices. This reduces the likelihood of individuals avoiding detection by disconnecting or disabling unauthorized WLAN devices.

There are also active WLAN scanning tools. Building on the information collected during passive scans, active scanning attempts to attach to discovered WLAN devices and conduct penetration or vulnerability-related testing. Organizations should be cautious in conducting active scans to make sure they do not inadvertently scan devices owned or operated by other organizations or individuals within range. It is important to evaluate the physical location of devices before actively scanning them. Generally, organizations should focus on identifying and locating potential rogue devices rather than performing active scans of such devices.

The types of tools mentioned in this section are examples of tools that are often effective at WLAN security monitoring. This is not intended to imply that no other types of tools may also be useful at WLAN security monitoring. What is important is having the necessary monitoring capabilities, not the labels applied to the tool or tools providing those capabilities.

3.3 Continuous Monitoring Recommendations

Organizations with WLANs should implement continuous monitoring solutions for their WLANs that provide all of the following detection capabilities:

- Unauthorized WLAN devices, including rogue APs and unauthorized client devices

- WLAN devices that are misconfigured or using weak WLAN protocols and protocol implementations

- Unusual WLAN usage patterns, such as extremely high numbers of client devices using a particular AP, abnormally high volumes of WLAN traffic involving a particular client device, or many failed attempts to join the WLAN in a short period of time

- The use of active WLAN scanners (e.g., war driving tools) that generate WLAN traffic. The use of passive sensors cannot be detected through monitoring controls.

- DoS attacks and conditions (e.g., network interference). Many denial of service attacks are detected by counting events during periods of time and alerting when threshold values are exceeded. For example, a large number of events involving the termination of WLAN sessions can indicate a DoS attack.

- Impersonation and man-in-the-middle attacks. For example, some WIDPS sensors can detect when a device is attempting to spoof the identity of another device.

Organizations with WLANs should also have the capability to identify the physical location of a detected WLAN threat by using triangulation—estimating the threat's approximate distance from multiple sensors by the strength of the threat's signal received by each sensor, then calculating the physical location at which the threat would be the estimated distance from each sensor. This allows an organization to send appropriate personnel, such as physical security staff, to the location to address the threat.

3.4   Periodic Assessment Recommendations

Organizations with WLANs should conduct regular periodic technical WLAN security assessments. These assessments should be performed at least annually to evaluate the overall security of the WLAN. In addition, organizations should perform periodic assessments at least quarterly unless continuous monitoring of WLAN security is already collecting all of the information about WLAN attacks and vulnerabilities needed for assessment purposes. For example, an organization that does not have comprehensive WIDPS coverage of its facilities should use mobile WIDPS sensors, WLAN scanners, or other tools with similar capabilities to search for rogue WLANs in areas outside the WIDPS's range.

The following are additional factors that organizations should consider when planning the frequency and breadth of periodic assessments:

- The location of the facility being scanned, because the physical proximity of a building to a public area (e.g., streets and public common areas) or its location in a busy metropolitan area may increase the risk of WLAN threats

- The security level of the data to be transmitted on the WLAN

- How often WLAN client devices connect to and disconnect from the environment, and the typical traffic levels for these devices (e.g., occasional activity or fairly constant activity)—this is because only active WLAN client devices are discoverable during a WLAN scan

- Physical changes to the facilities, such as construction projects that could affect the strength and propagation of WLAN signals

Appendix A—Supporting NIST SP 800-53 Security Controls and Publications

The major controls in the NIST Special Publication 800-53, *Recommended Security Controls for Federal Information Systems and Organizations* control catalog that affect an organization's wireless local area network (WLAN) security are:

AC-3, Access Enforcement

Related controls: AC-2, AC-4, AC-5, AC-6, AC-16, AC-17, AC-18, AC-19, AC-20, AC-21, AC-22, AU-9, CM-5, CM-6, MA-3, MA-4, MA-5, SA-7, SC-13, SI-9

AC-4, Information Flow Enforcement

Related controls: AC-17, AC-19, AC-21, CM-7, SA-8, SC-2, SC-5, SC-7, SC-18

AC-18, Wireless Access

Related controls: AC-3, IA-2, IA-3, IA-8

References: NIST Special Publications 800-48, 800-94, 800-97

AC-19, Access Control for Mobile Devices

Related controls: MP-4, MP-5

References: NIST Special Publications 800-114, 800-124

AC-20, Use of External Information Systems

Related controls: AC-3, AC-17, PL-4

References: FIPS Publication 199

CA-2, Security Assessments

Related controls: CA-6, CA-7, PM-9, SA-11

References: FIPS Publication 199; NIST Special Publications 800-37, 800-53A, 800-115

CA-7, Continuous Monitoring

Related controls: CA-2, CA-5, CA-6, CM-3, CM-4

References: NIST Special Publications 800-37, 800-53A; US-CERT Technical Cyber Security Alerts; DOD Information Assurance Vulnerability Alerts

CM-6, Configuration Settings

Related controls: CM-2, CM-3, SI-4

References: OMB Memoranda 07-11, 07-18, 08-22; NIST Special Publications 800-70, 800-128; Web: nvd.nist.gov; www.nsa.gov)

AU-2, Auditable Events

Related control: AU-3

References: NIST Special Publication 800-92

IA-2, Identification and Authentication (Organizational Users)

Related controls: AC-14, AC-17, AC-18, IA-4, IA-5

References: HSPD 12; OMB Memorandum 04-04; FIPS Publication 201; NIST Special Publications

800-63, 800-73, 800-76, 800-78

IA-3, Device Identification and Authentication

Related controls: AC-17, AC-18

IA-5, Authenticator Management

Related controls: AC-2, IA-2, PL-4, PS-6

References: OMB Memorandum 04-04; FIPS Publication 201; NIST Special Publications 800-73, 800-63, 800-76, 800-78

IA-8, Identification and Authentication (Non-Organizational Users)

Related controls: AC-14, AC-17, AC-18, MA-4

References: OMB Memorandum 04-04; Web: www.cio.gov/eauthentication; NIST Special Publication 800-63

PE-18, Location of Information System Components

RA-3, Risk Assessment

Reference: NIST Special Publication 800-30

RA-5, Vulnerability Scanning

Related controls: CA-2, CM-6, RA-3, SI-2

References: NIST Special Publications 800-40, 800-70, 800-115; Web: cwe.mitre.org; nvd.nist.gov

SC-7, Boundary Protection

Related controls: AC-4, IR-4, SC-5

References: FIPS Publication 199; NIST Special Publications 800-41, 800-77

SC-8, Transmission Integrity

Related controls: AC-17, PE-4

References: FIPS Publications 140-2, 197; NIST Special Publications 800-52, 800-77, 800-81, 800-113; NSTISSI No. 7003

SC-9, Transmission Confidentiality

Related controls: AC-17, PE-4

References: FIPS Publications 140-2, 197; NIST Special Publications 800-52, 800-77, 800-113; CNSS Policy 15; NSTISSI No. 7003

SI-2, Flaw Remediation

Related controls: CA-2, CA-7, CM-3, MA-2, IR-4, RA-5, SA-11, SI-11

References: NIST Special Publication 800-40

SI-4, Information System Monitoring

Related controls: AC-4, AC-8, AC-17, AU-2, AU-6, SI-3, SI-7

References: NIST Special Publications 800-61, 800-83, 800-92, 800-94

Information on these controls and guidelines on possible implementations can be found in the following publications:

- *SP 800-30, Risk Management Guide for Information Technology Systems*
- *Draft SP 800-30 Revision 1, Guide for Conducting Risk Assessments*
- *SP 800-37, Guide for Applying the Risk Management Framework to Federal Information Systems: A Security Life Cycle Approach*
- *SP 800-40 Version 2.0, Creating a Patch and Vulnerability Management Program*
- *SP 800-41 Rev. 1, Guidelines on Firewalls and Firewall Policy*
- *SP 800-48 Rev. 1, Guide to Securing Legacy IEEE 802.11 Wireless Networks*
- *SP 800-52, Guidelines for the Selection and Use of Transport Layer Security (TLS) Implementations*
- *SP 800-53 Rev. 3, Recommended Security Controls for Federal Information Systems and Organizations*
- *SP 800-53A Rev. 1, Guide for Assessing the Security Controls in Federal Information Systems and Organizations*
- *SP 800-61 Rev. 1, Computer Security Incident Handling Guide*
- *SP 800-63 Rev. 1: E-Authentication Guideline*
- *SP 800-70 Rev. 2, National Checklist Program for IT Products--Guidelines for Checklist Users and Developers*
- *SP 800-73-3, Interfaces for Personal Identity Verification*
- *Draft SP 800-76-2, Biometric Data Specification for Personal Identity Verification*
- *SP 800-77, Guide to IPsec VPNs*
- *SP 800-78-3, Cryptographic Algorithms and Key Sizes for Personal Identification Verification (PIV)*
- *SP 800-81 Rev. 1, Secure Domain Name System (DNS) Deployment Guide*
- *SP 800-83, Guide to Malware Incident Prevention and Handling*
- *SP 800-92, Guide to Computer Security Log Management*
- *SP 800-94, Guide to Intrusion Detection and Prevention Systems (IDPS)*
- *SP 800-97, Establishing Wireless Robust Security Networks: A Guide to IEEE 802.11i*
- *SP 800-113, Guide to SSL VPNs*
- *SP 800-114, User's Guide to Securing External Devices for Telework and Remote Access*
- *SP 800-115, Technical Guide to Information Security Testing and Assessment*
- *SP 800-124, Guidelines on Cell Phone and PDA Security*
- *SP 800-128, Guide for Security-Focused Configuration Management of Information Systems*

Appendix B—Acronyms and Abbreviations

Selected acronyms and abbreviations used in the guide are defined below.

AP	Access Point
BIOS	Basic Input/Output System
DHS	Department of Homeland Security
DISA	Defense Information Systems Agency
DoS	Denial of Service
DS	Distribution System
FISMA	Federal Information Security Management Act
GAO	Government Accountability Office
IDPS	Intrusion Detection and Prevention System
IEEE	Institute of Electrical and Electronics Engineers
IT	Information Technology
ITL	Information Technology Laboratory
LAN	Local Area Network
NIST	National Institute of Standards and Technology
OMB	Office of Management and Budget
OS	Operating System
SP	Special Publication
STIG	Security Technical Implementation Guide
TIC	Trusted Internet Connection
USB	Universal Serial Bus
WIDPS	Wireless Intrusion Detection and Prevention System
WiMAX	Worldwide Interoperability for Microwave Access
WLAN	Wireless Local Area Network

Appendix C—References

The list below provides references for the publication.

[GAO-11-43]   GAO-11-43, *Federal Agencies Have Taken Steps to Secure Wireless Networks, but Further Actions Can Mitigate Risk*, November 2010. http://www.gao.gov/new.items/d1143.pdf

[NCP]   National Checklist Program Repository. http://checklists.nist.gov/

[SP800-37]   NIST Special Publication 800-37 Revision 1, *Guide for Applying the Risk Management Framework to Federal Information Systems: A Security Life Cycle Approach*, February 2010. http://csrc.nist.gov/publications/PubsSPs.html#800-37

[SP800-48]   NIST Special Publication 800-48 Revision 1, *Guide to Securing Legacy IEEE 802.11 Wireless Networks*, July 2008. http://csrc.nist.gov/publications/PubsSPs.html#800-48

[SP800-53]   NIST Special Publication 800-53 Revision 3, *Recommended Security Controls for Federal Information Systems and Organizations*, August 2009. http://csrc.nist.gov/publications/PubsSPs.html#800-53

[SP800-53A]   NIST Special Publication 800-53A, *Guide for Assessing the Security Controls in Federal Information Systems and Organizations: Building Effective Security Assessment Plans*, June 2010. http://csrc.nist.gov/publications/PubsSPs.html#800-53a

[SP800-70]   NIST Special Publication 800-70 Revision 2, *National Checklist Program for IT Products—Guidelines for Checklist Users and Developers*, February 2011. http://csrc.nist.gov/publications/PubsSPs.html#800-70

[SP800-94]   NIST Special Publication 800-94, *Guide to Intrusion Detection and Prevention Systems (IDPS)*, February 2007. http://csrc.nist.gov/publications/PubsSPs.html#800-94

[SP800-97]   NIST Special Publication 800-97, *Establishing Robust Security Networks: A Guide to IEEE 802.11i*, February 2007. http://csrc.nist.gov/publications/PubsSPs.html#800-97

[SP800-115]   NIST Special Publication 800-115, *Technical Guide to Information Security Testing and Assessment*, September 2008. http://csrc.nist.gov/publications/PubsSPs.html#800-115

[SP800-137]   NIST Special Publication 800-137, *Information Security Continuous Monitoring for Federal Information Systems and Organizations*, September 2011. http://csrc.nist.gov/publications/PubsSPs.html#800-137